How did ancient Rome become an empire? Where did ancient Romans go for fun? What happened to the Roman town of Pompeii? What have we learned from it?

Find out the answers to these questions and more in . . .

Magic Tree House® Research Guide

ANCIENT ROME AND POMPEII

A nonfiction companion to *Vacation Under the Volcano*

It's Jack and Annie's very own guide to the fascinating history of ancient Rome and Pompeii!

Including:

- Roman war machines
- Famous Romans
- The eruption of Mt. Vesuvius
- Gladiators

And much more!

Here's what people are saying about the Magic Tree House® Research Guides:

Your Research Guides are a great addition to the Magic Tree House series! I have used Rain Forests *and* Space *as "read-alouds" during science units. Thank you for these!!*—Cheryl M., teacher

My eight-year-old son thinks your books are great—and I agree. I wish my high school students had read the Research Guides when they were his age.
—John F., parent and teacher

And from the Magic Tree House® Web site:

My son loves the Research Guides about knights, pirates, and mummies. He has even asked for a notebook, which he takes with him to the museum for his research.—A parent

The Research Guides have been very helpful to us, as our daughter has an abundance of questions. Please come out with more. They help us help her find the answers to her questions!—An appreciative mom and dad

I love your books. I have a great library at home filled with your books and Research Guides. The [Knights and Castles] *Research Guide really helped me do a report on castles and knights!*—A young reader

Magic Tree House®
Research Guide

ANCIENT ROME AND POMPEII

A nonfiction companion to
Vacation Under the Volcano

by Mary Pope Osborne
and Natalie Pope Boyce

illustrated by Sal Murdocca

SCHOLASTIC INC.
New York Toronto London Auckland Sydney
Mexico City New Delhi Hong Kong Buenos Aires

ISBN-13: 978-0-439-89500-2
ISBN-10: 0-439-89500-6

Published by Scholastic Inc., 557 Broadway, New York, NY 10012, by arrangement with Random House Children's Books, a division of Random House, Inc.

12 11 10 9 8 7 6 5 4 3 2 1 6 7 8 9 10 11/0

Printed in the U.S.A. 40

First Scholastic printing, September 2006

www.magictreehouse.com

For Susan Longfellow

Historical Consultant:
JOHN MUCCIGROSSO, Associate Professor of Classics, Drew University.

Education Consultant:
HEIDI JOHNSON, Earth Science and Paleontology, Lowell Junior High School, Bisbee, Arizona.

Very special thanks as usual to Paul Coughlin for the wonderful photographs; and to the excellent team at Random House: Joanne Yates Russell, Gloria Cheng, Angela Roberts, and Mallory Loehr; and especially to our patient and really smart editor, Diane Landolf.

ANCIENT ROME AND POMPEII

Contents

Dear Readers,

When we began to work on this book, we found there was so much to learn about ancient Rome. We knew about the gladiators and Pompeii and some other things. But suddenly the story of 2,000 years of Roman history had to be told!

We got big, thick notebooks. We grabbed our pencils and headed to the library. Whole shelves of books on ancient Rome were waiting for us. We learned about the great Roman army. We read about the rulers and heroes of Rome. We

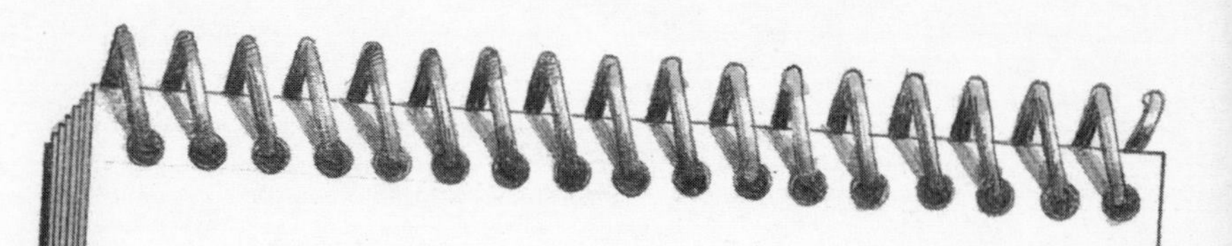

even looked at pictures that showed old Roman roads . . . some are still used today!

Then we went home and sat down at the computer. There were great Web sites just waiting to be explored. So put on your gladiator's helmet and come join us. We're off to ancient Rome!

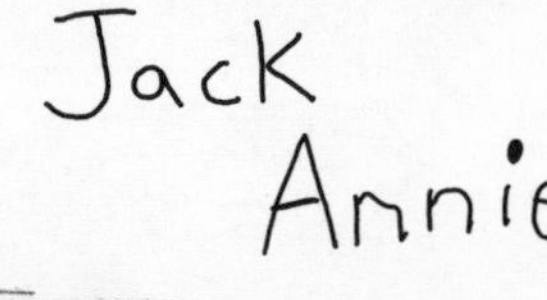

1

Ancient Rome

The story of Rome begins with a legend. According to the legend, the god Mars had twin boys named Romulus and Remus. The boys were abandoned on the banks of the river Tiber. A wolf found the babies and nursed them like a mother with her own milk. Later, a kind shepherd took them home to his wife and raised the boys as his sons.

When Romulus and Remus grew up, they decided to build a city on the spot where they had been found. A fight broke out over who would be in charge of the city. Romulus killed Remus. Legend has it that Romulus went on to found the city of Rome and named it for himself.

The real story of ancient Rome is a bit different. Rome was actually founded over 3,000 years ago. Farmers and fishermen settled on hills near the river Tiber in what is now Italy. These small hill settlements grew into a town.

The river Tiber helped the village grow. Salt marshes surrounded parts of the river near the town. Salt was a valuable trading item. The Romans traveled up and down the river, trading salt and other goods with neighboring tribes.

This woodcut illustrates an ancient Roman trading ship.

The Romans formed a small army. They began to fight for the land of other groups in the region. At first, the battles were small. But as the Romans gained land and power, all of Italy fell under Roman control. As the years passed, the armies of Rome went on to conquer Greece and the peoples living in what is now Austria and France. In less than 300 years, the Romans had conquered most of western Europe. They also conquered Britain and much of North Africa and the Middle East.

Roman lands spread out over two and a half million square miles. The people the Romans ruled included Egyptians, Jews, Greeks, Germans, Celts, and Syrians.

753–509 BC: Age of Kings

Stories tell us that in the beginning, ancient Rome was ruled by kings. Many people believe that was true. The kings' rule may have lasted for over 200 years. But the Romans were unhappy with their last king, Tarquin. They overthrew him and set up a republic. From then on, the Romans never wanted another king as their ruler.

509–31 BC: Roman Republic

A republic is a form of government where no one person has complete control. In the Roman Republic, the people had some say in their government. They elected two men called *consuls* to replace the king. The consuls could only hold office for one year. Both men had to agree on every decision.

The government also included a group of powerful men called *senators*. Senators served in the *Senate* and advised the consuls. By the end of the

This statue of the consul Cicero is in a museum in Oxford, U.K.

In the beginning, the Senate had 300 members. Later, there were as many as 800.

fourth century BC, senators served for life.

Ordinary citizens served together in groups called *assemblies* (uh-SEM-bleez). The assemblies met at least once a year to elect public officials and whenever they needed to pass laws. Women and slaves and people who were not from Rome could not vote.

27 BC–AD 476: Age of Emperors

It was dangerous to be a Roman emperor. Many were murdered by their enemies.

After the republic ended, *emperors* (EM-pur-urz) ruled Rome. An emperor was like a king with great powers. Some emperors were worshiped like gods. The Senate and the assemblies still existed, but the emperor was really in charge.

After an emperor died, one of his relatives usually became the next emperor.

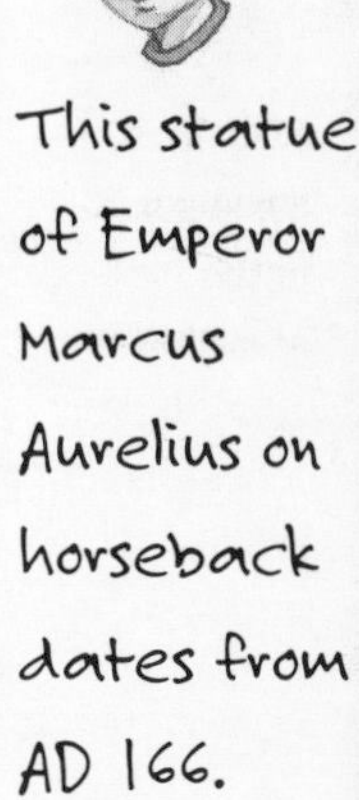

This statue of Emperor Marcus Aurelius on horseback dates from AD 166.

The Romans

In ancient Rome, people were divided into three groups: *patricians* (puh-TRIH-shunz), *plebeians* (pluh-BEE-unz), and *slaves*. Patricians were rich citizens who owned land and had many slaves. Many patricians were powerful leaders in government or the military.

Plebeians could serve in the assemblies.

The plebeians were not patricians. They were mostly ordinary Roman citizens such as shopkeepers and craftsmen. Some plebeians were wealthy. But in the beginning of the republic, they did not have as much power as the patricians.

There were also many poor plebeians in Rome without jobs. They depended on the charity of the patricians.

For many years, the plebeians resented the power of the patricians. They wanted more say in the government. Later, plebeians were allowed to become consuls and gained much of the power that only the patricians once had.

Slaves made up a large part of the population. They had no rights and were not allowed to vote. Although some families treated their slaves almost like family, some slaves lived hard lives. Many did not have much education, but others did and acted as tutors to the family. Many slaves were captured in wars or sold by their poor parents for money. Slaves could save money and buy their own freedom.

Wealthy families owned as many as 500 slaves.

This Roman lady has slaves to do her hair, hold her mirror, and dress her.

Map of
Ancient Roman Empire
Britain
Gaul
Atlantic
Ocean
Adriatic Sea
Rome
Italy
Pompeii
Spain
Sicily
Carthage
North Africa

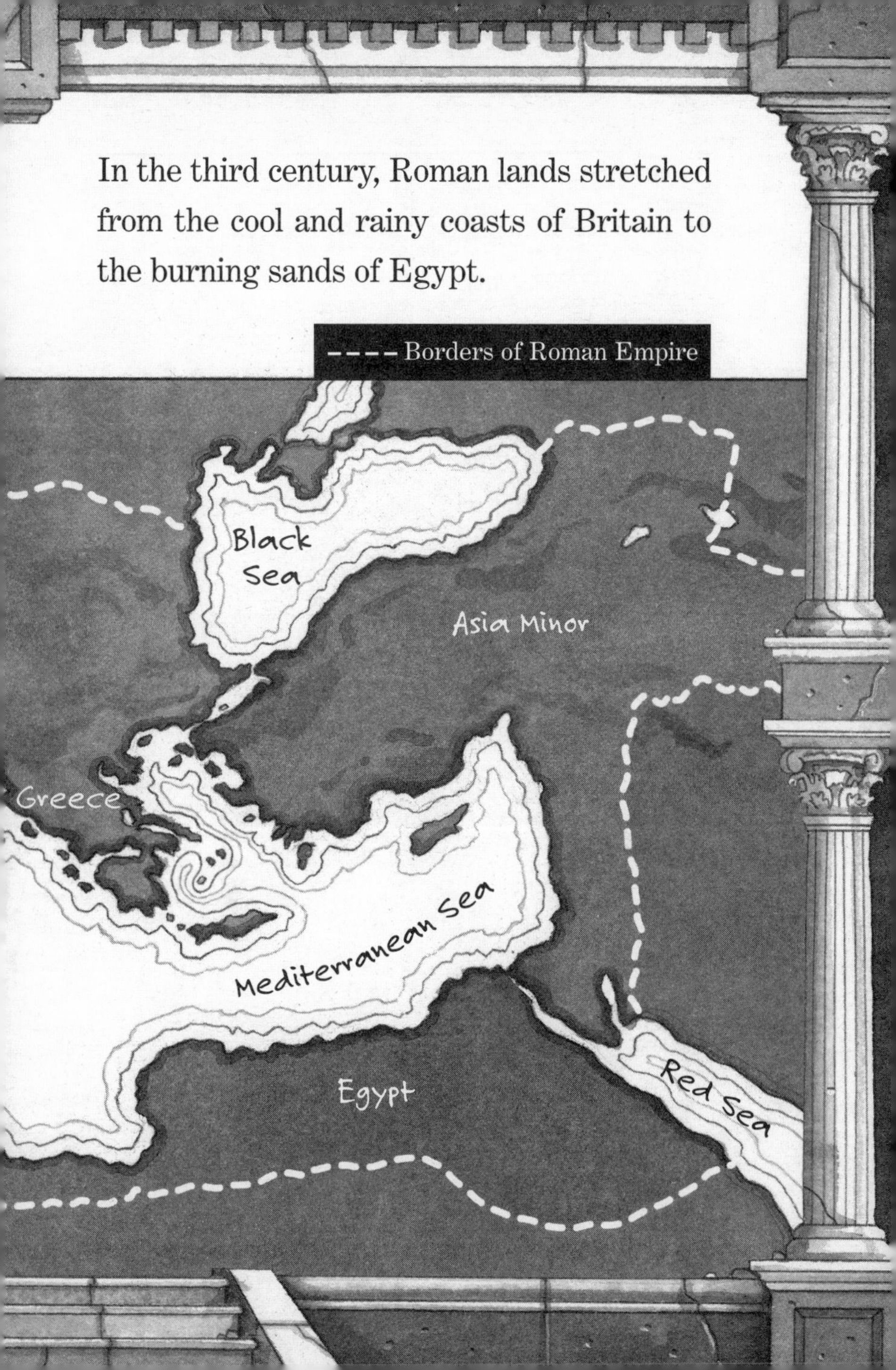
In the third century, Roman lands stretched from the cool and rainy coasts of Britain to the burning sands of Egypt.

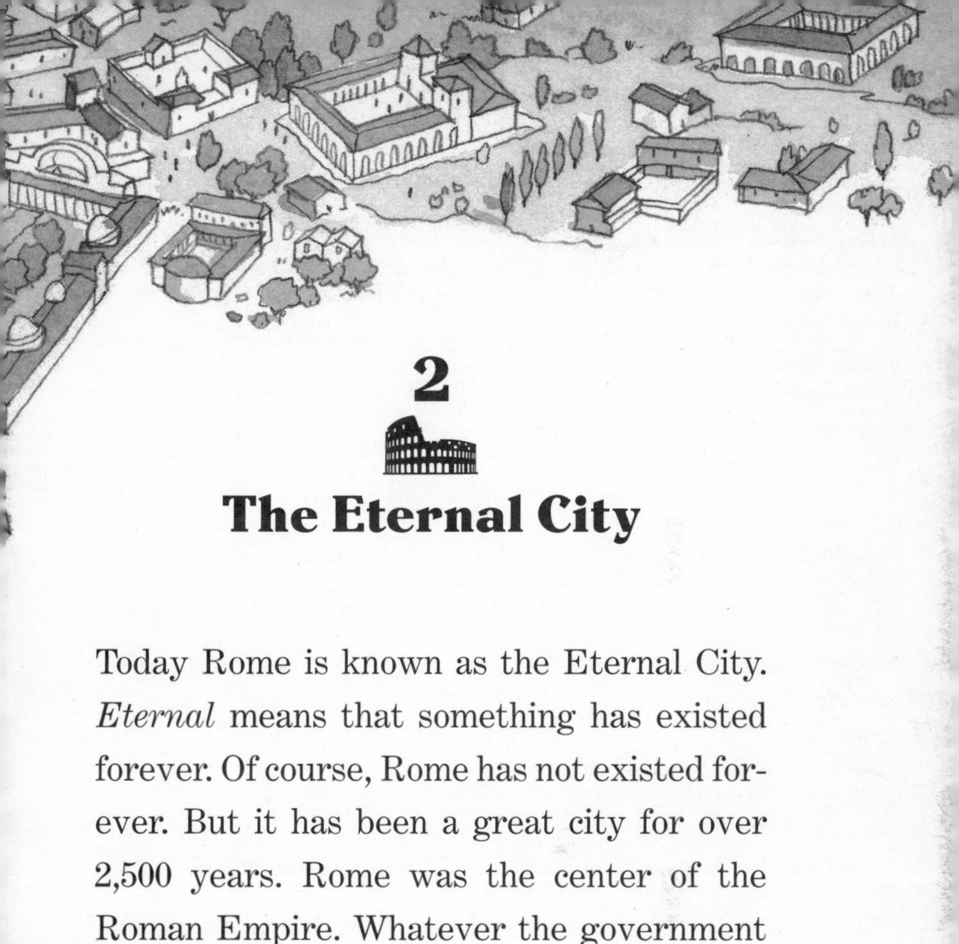

2

The Eternal City

Today Rome is known as the Eternal City. *Eternal* means that something has existed forever. Of course, Rome has not existed forever. But it has been a great city for over 2,500 years. Rome was the center of the Roman Empire. Whatever the government in Rome decided was obeyed throughout the empire.

The streets of ancient Rome were crowded

At one time there were over 46,000 apartment buildings in Rome.

Architects plan and design buildings.

with apartment houses, shops, and bars. There were also beautiful monuments, public buildings, temples, bridges, and glorious fountains. The ancient Romans were master builders. Some Roman buildings have lasted for over 2,000 years!

Romans borrowed many ideas from the Greeks. In fact, they often hired Greek *architects* (AR-kuh-tektz) to plan their buildings. But the Romans also invented new ways of building things themselves.

Roman buildings often had strong, rounded arches and beautiful domes. The Romans also built sturdy bridges, roads, and tunnels.

They used a new building material called *concrete.* In fact, the Romans invented concrete around 200 BC.

Roman arch

Workers made concrete by mixing cement, sand, gravel, and water together. When the mixture hardened, it became very strong. Roman buildings were sometimes stronger and taller than those in Greece. In Rome today, remains of these ancient buildings are reminders of the glory that was Rome.

Sometimes the architect's name was chiseled on a stone that went into the building.

The Colosseum

An <u>amphitheater</u> is an outdoor stadium with rows of seats.

The Colosseum (kah-luh-SEE-um) was a gigantic outdoor *amphitheater* (AM-fuh-thee-uh-tur), a lot like a football stadium. It stood around 160 feet high and held over 50,000 people!

But there was no football on this field. Romans went to the Colosseum to see bloody sports—sports where people and animals died terrible deaths. Crowds cheered as they watched staged battles.

Gladiators were men trained to fight for the amusement of crowds.

In one battle alone, 10,000 people are said to have died! People also watched as *gladiators* (GLA-dee-ay-turz) fought one another or wild animals.

Roman rulers provided free entertainment to keep the people happy. When the Colosseum opened in AD 80, Emperor Titus ordered a hundred days of games to be held. Thousands of animals and gladiators died. The Roman crowds loved all of it.

Aqueducts

At one time, there were over a million people in Rome. They needed water for cooking, bathing, and drinking. Roman builders made *aqueducts* (A-kwuh-duktz) to deliver water to them.

Aqua means "water" in Latin.

Aqueducts are channels that carry water from distant springs. In ancient Rome, eleven aqueducts carried water over a total of 260 miles. Although it's hard to believe, a few of Rome's ancient aqueducts are still in use today.

This aqueduct in Nîmes, France, was built over a deep gorge.

Most of the water flowed through underground channels. But some aqueducts went aboveground. They carried water over hills and valleys and looked like tall bridges held up by high arches.

Some aqueducts carried water from 57 miles away!

When the water reached the city, it flowed into huge containers. Pipes carried the water from the containers into various parts of the city. The pipes were made of stone, terra-cotta, wood, leather, lead, and bronze.

Pantheon

The word <u>pantheon</u> means "of all gods."

Romans worshiped many different gods. The *Pantheon* (PAN-thee-ahn) was a temple dedicated to all the gods.

The Pantheon is in good condition today. And yet it was built nearly 2,000 years ago. The Romans used a super-strong concrete when they built it. They wanted it to last—and it did!

A huge dome sits atop the Pantheon. In fact, until modern times, it was the largest dome on any building ever! The top of the dome is covered in bronze. It shimmers in the sunlight and, in ancient times, could be seen all over Rome.

Today the Pantheon is a Christian church. People stand in the same spot where ancient Romans stood to worship their gods.

The Forum Romanum

Near the Colosseum stand the ruins of a once-great public square. This was the famous Forum Romanum, the center of Roman life. Shops, offices, and monuments lined the square.

The Forum was a favorite place for making speeches. The ancient Romans were proud of their ability to make speeches. *Orators* (OR-uh-turz), or speakers, held forth as crowds gathered to listen.

The word <u>orator</u> comes from the Latin <u>orare</u>, which means "to speak."

When the Roman Empire came to an end, so did the Forum. Animals grazed in its ruins. Farmers grew vegetables where once-proud Romans conducted business. And today we only see hints of what the great Forum Romanum must have been.

The remains of the Forum Romanum can still be seen today.

Baths of Caracalla

Most Romans did not have bathrooms at home. They used pots for toilets or public bathrooms. Public bathrooms had rows of stone benches with openings cut into them. Running water below the benches carried away the sewage.

Urine was saved and used to dye cloth or tan leather!

Yuck! The Romans brushed their teeth with powdered mouse brains!

Romans got drinking water from street fountains. They went to public baths to bathe and meet their friends. At one time, there were 900 public baths in ancient Rome! Some were small, but others were huge. Some baths stayed open twenty-four hours a day. One was lighted with 1,000 lamps.

The Baths of Caracalla could hold over 1,600 people. Exquisite marble and colorful mosaics covered the walls and floors. Gardens with splashing fountains surrounded the buildings. Visitors to the baths enjoyed art galleries, libraries, and restaurants.

Inside the baths, bathers soaked in either warm or cold water. Water was heated by furnaces under the floor called *hypocausts* (HI-puh-kostz). Slaves stood by to hand out towels and fragrant oils as bathers moved from one pool to another.

In Rome today, people still visit the Baths of Caracalla. But now they go at night to listen to glorious concerts under the stars.

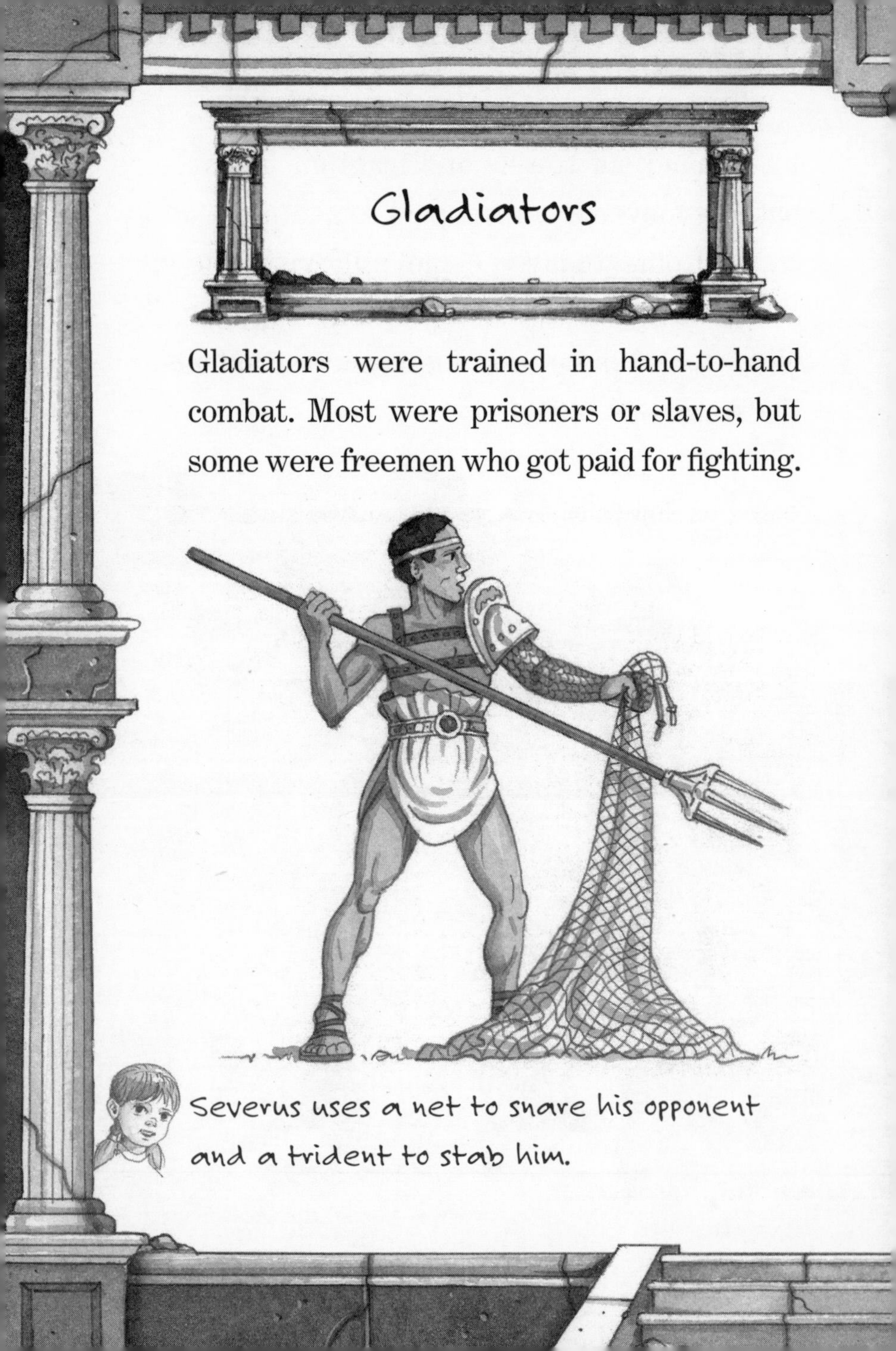

Gladiators

Gladiators were trained in hand-to-hand combat. Most were prisoners or slaves, but some were freemen who got paid for fighting.

Severus uses a net to snare his opponent and a trident to stab him.

Gladiators usually fought to the death. But if an especially brave fighter was wounded, the emperor could spare his life. The eager crowds bet on their favorites. Some gladiators got as much attention as rock stars do today!

Marcus fights with a sword and a shield.

3

The Roman Military

In AD 103, huge crowds lined the streets of Rome. They'd come to see the return of Emperor Trajan after his victory over the Dacians.

Trumpets rang out. People moved forward to catch a glimpse as standard-bearers strode by carrying flags with symbols identifying their units. Hundreds of soldiers paraded by, loaded with treasures from the defeated people. Next a bedraggled group

of prisoners shuffled by, dragging their chains.

And finally Trajan himself rode by in a golden chariot pulled by four prancing horses. The Roman army had returned in triumph once again!

Men ages 17–46 could be soldiers.

For over 400 years, Rome had one of the greatest armies the world has ever seen. At the peak of the empire, 300,000 soldiers swore absolute loyalty to the emperor and to their generals. The Roman Empire would not have been possible without the army.

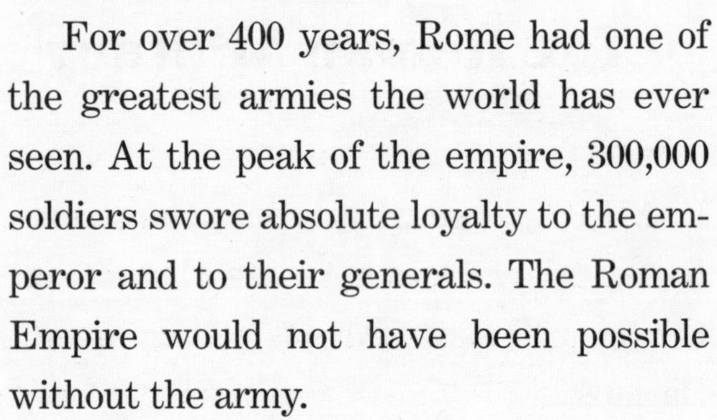

The Legion

Roman soldiers belonged to fighting groups made up of about 6,000 men. These groups were called *legions* (LEE-junz). Legions were divided into eighty-man units called *centuries* (SEN-chuh-reez). Centuries were commanded by battle-hardened officers called *centurions* (sen-CHUR-ee-unz).

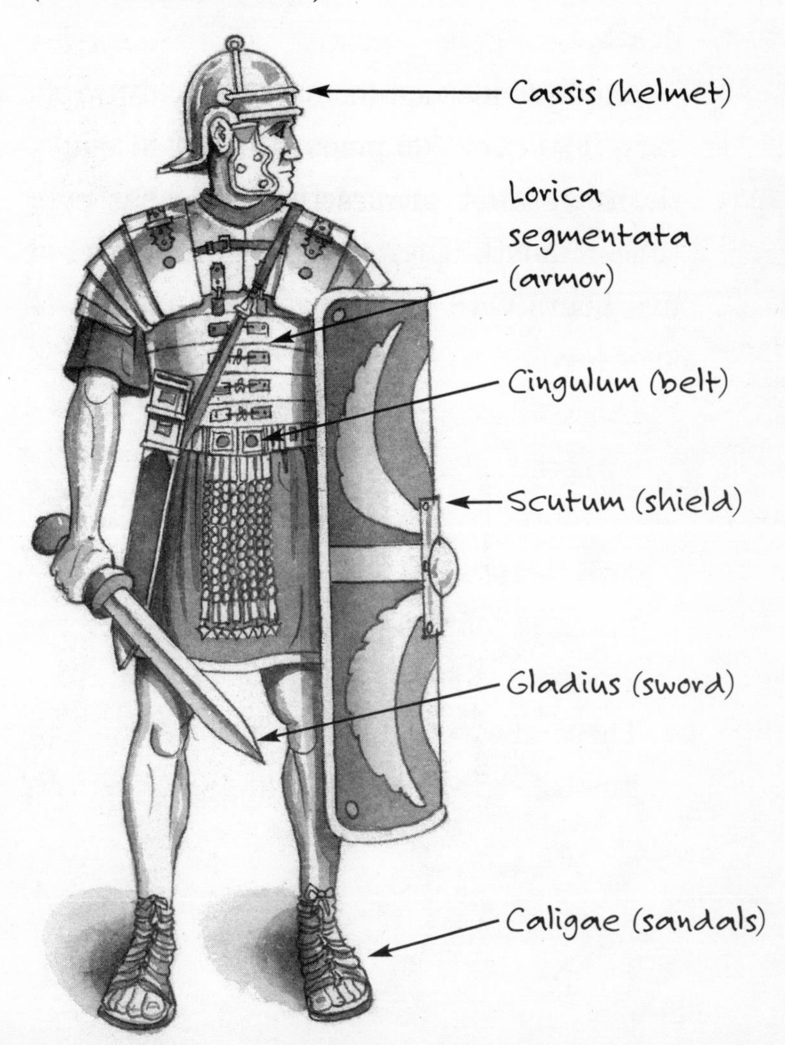

Training

Centurions were responsible for training their men. The training was strict and brutal. Punishment included beatings and even death.

Soldiers learned to march quickly while carrying heavy equipment. To stay in shape, the men went on practice marches three times a month. They covered twenty miles in five hours with more than sixty pounds of gear.

Centurions turned their men into skillful and deadly fighters. Victory depended on their ability to cut and thrust with a sword, shoot arrows from a bow, throw a javelin, and use a sling. To develop strength, soldiers practiced with swords twice as heavy as the ones they used in battle.

Soldiers drilled twice a day with both swords and shields.

Soldiers carried several short and long javelins into battle. Like the swords, practice javelins were much heavier. Other weapons they trained with daily included bows and arrows.

All this training paid off. Fighting came so naturally to them that one writer who saw the Romans in battle said it looked as if their weapons were attached to their bodies.

Soldiers gained extra muscle by throwing heavy stones.

Besides weapons training, soldiers

Roman armies sometimes took war elephants and dogs into battle.

learned to swim well so they could cross streams and rivers. They also learned to dig trenches, build bridges, and erect forts.

Battle Formations

Romans sometimes fought in a formation called a *testudo*, or *tortoise* (TOR-tus)

formation. A tortoise is a turtle. Men in the front lines stood side by side. They held their shields up in front of them.

The soldiers behind them held their shields over the men in front. The shields protected them from the enemy's arrows and spears. The soldiers felt as safe as a turtle in its shell!

Soldiers wore long red cloaks into battle. Their enemies saw a sea of red.

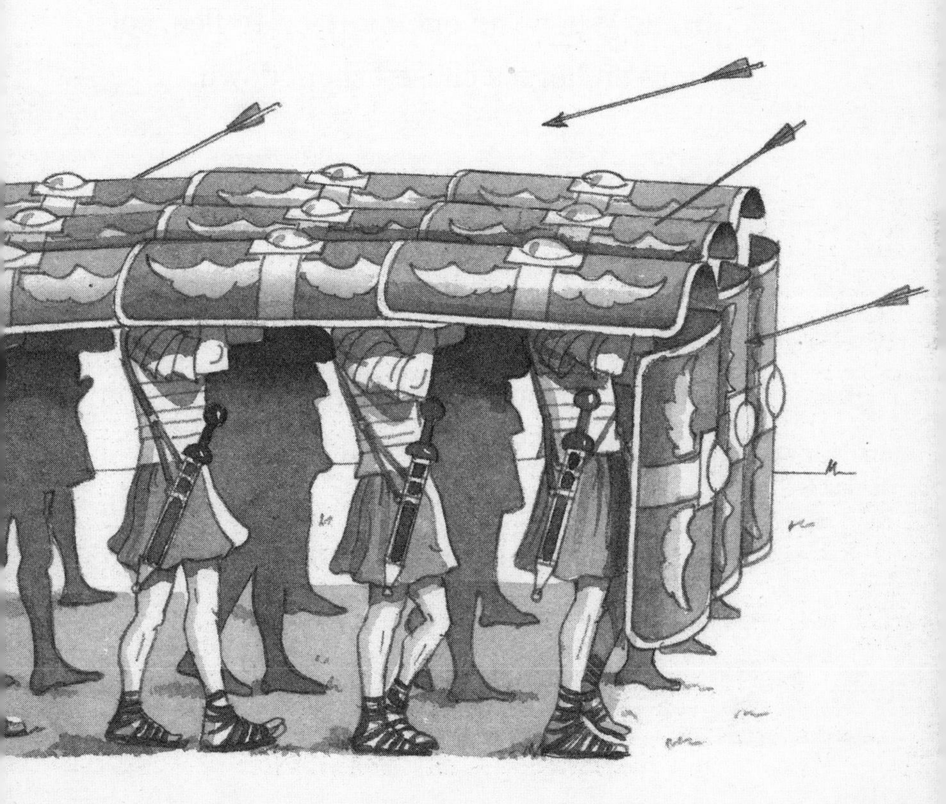

Soldiers fought about three feet apart.

When the battle began, trumpets rang out. This alerted the men to advance. At exactly the right moment, the men ran quickly forward and hurled their javelins.

Hand-to-hand combat often followed. As fighting dragged on, fresh soldiers in the rear replaced tired soldiers in the front. When the enemy tried to flee, soldiers on horses chased them down.

Caesar Captures a City

Romans excelled at *siege* (SEEJ) warfare. A siege is when one army surrounds and attacks a town or fort. In 52 BC, Julius Caesar's army began a siege on Avaricum, a walled town in Gaul.

Avaricum was in what is now France.

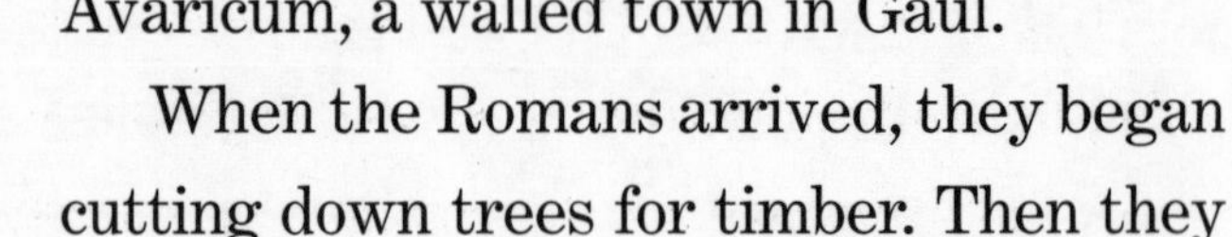

When the Romans arrived, they began cutting down trees for timber. Then they built shelters for protection from arrows and spears.

Inside the shelters, the men quickly constructed ramps and siege towers.

In the tortoise formation, they dragged the ramps up to the base of the wall. Then they rolled the towers up the ramps. The men climbed up the towers to fight their way across the wall. But the people inside the town put up their own towers. They shot burning arrows and hurled rocks.

Soldiers often shot arrows tipped with burning rags.

The battle raged for twenty-five days and nights. Finally, Roman towers rose twenty feet over the city walls! The Roman soldiers clambered over the walls. Once inside, they opened the gates to the town. Roman troops poured in. Death and destruction rained down upon the Gauls.

As the empire grew, so did the need

for a strong army. As one Roman military writer said, "He who wants peace should be ready for war." The powerful Romans were always ready for war.

Roman Seige Warfare

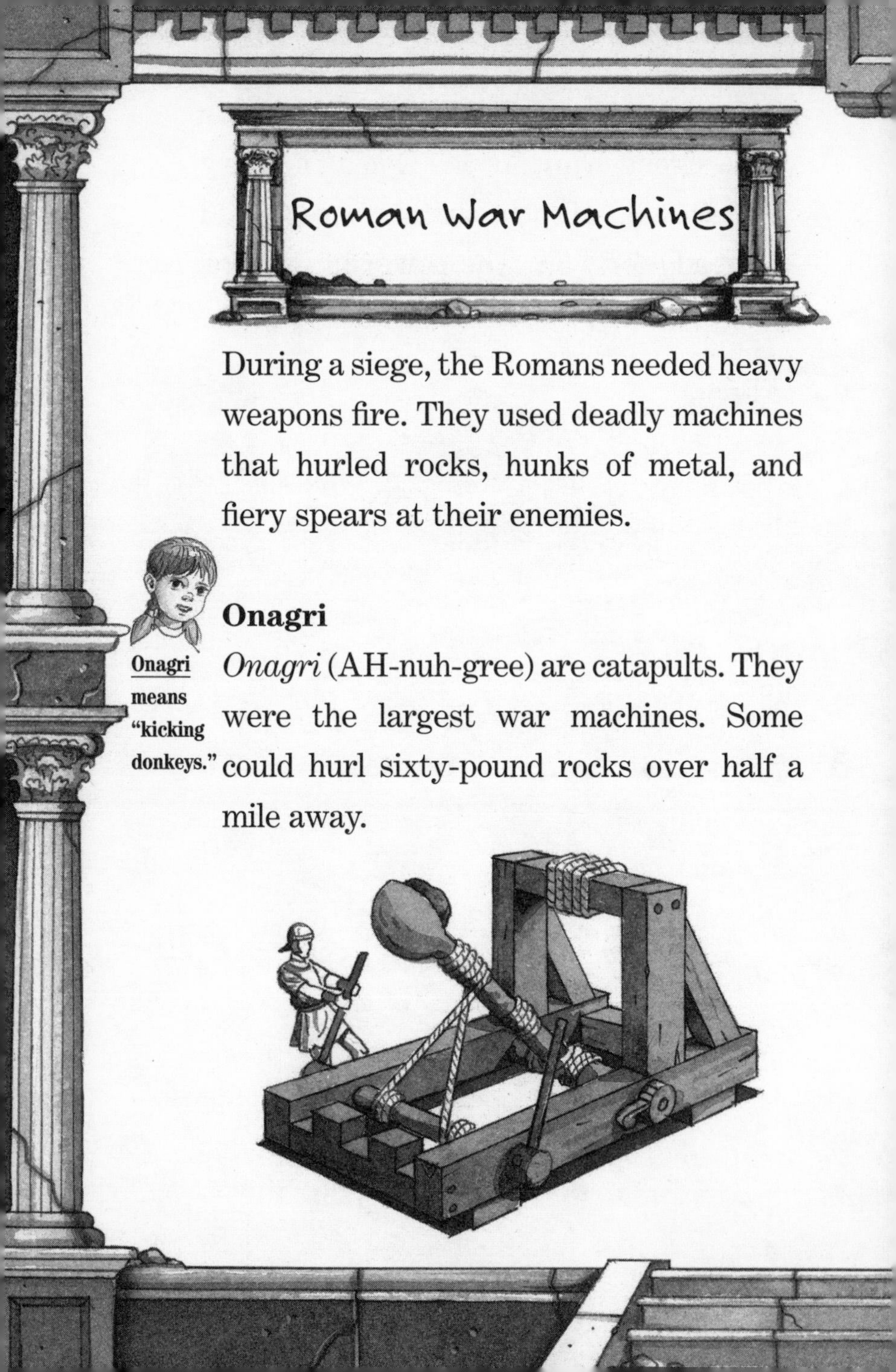

Roman War Machines

During a siege, the Romans needed heavy weapons fire. They used deadly machines that hurled rocks, hunks of metal, and fiery spears at their enemies.

Onagri

Onagri (AH-nuh-gree) are catapults. They were the largest war machines. Some could hurl sixty-pound rocks over half a mile away.

Onagri means "kicking donkeys."

Flamethrowers

Flamethrowers shot twelve-foot burning darts up to 2,000 feet away!

Ballista

A *ballista* (buh-LEES-tuh) is a kind of crossbow. The largest needed ten men to operate. Soldiers loaded it with rocks or pointed metal bolts that shot out at about 115 miles an hour! Anything in their path was immediately destroyed.

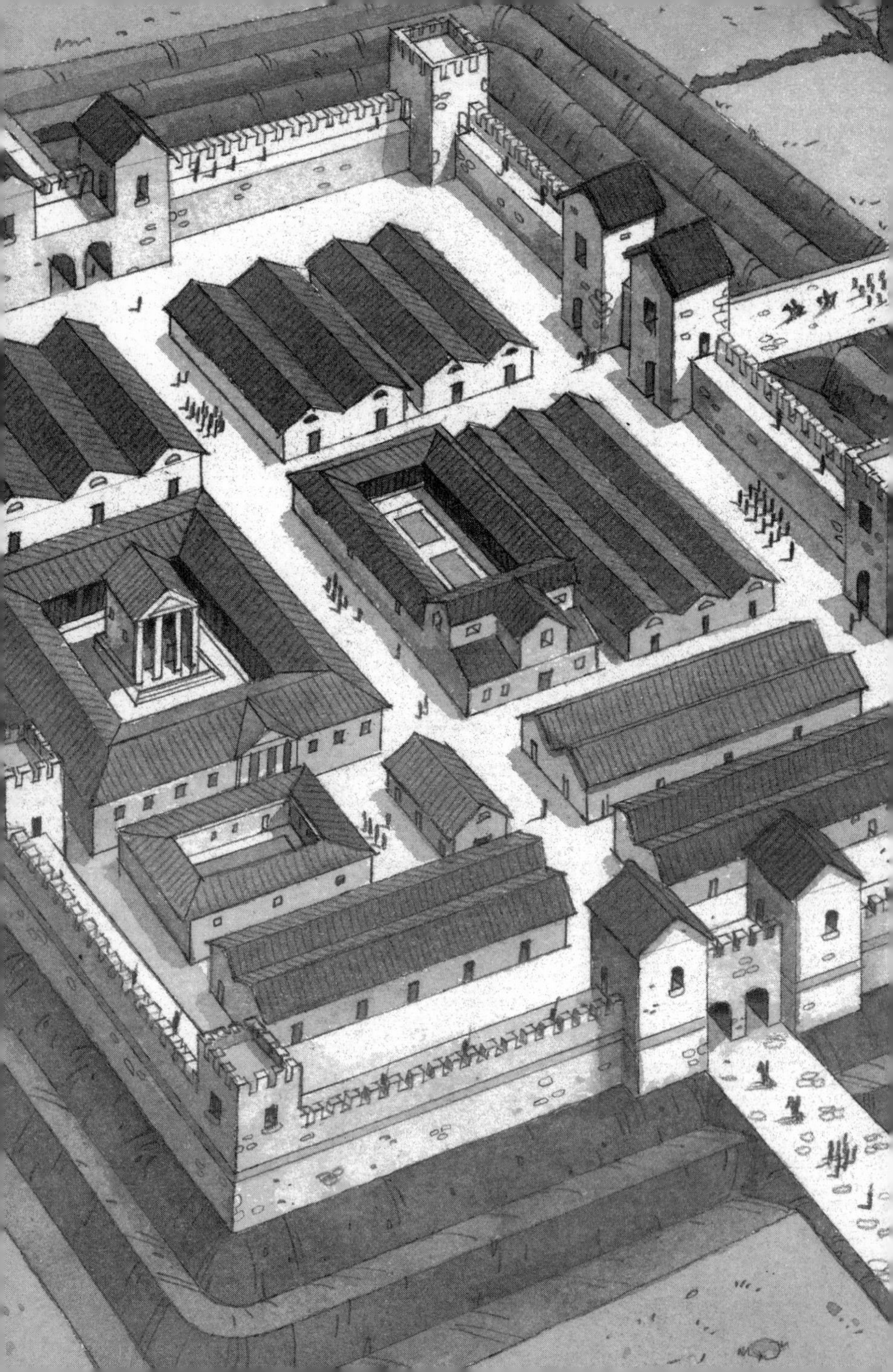

4

Uniting the Empire

The Roman Empire was at its strongest around AD 117. Parts of the empire, like Greece and Egypt, had long histories of their own. The Romans allowed almost everyone to keep their own languages, customs, and religions.

The Romans were famous for creating order wherever they went. Everyone had to obey Roman laws and to pay taxes. At times people rebelled and made it difficult to maintain law and order. The Romans needed to make sure the empire remained united. They accomplished this in many different ways.

When they conquered a region, the Romans built Roman forts in the area. Soldiers in the forts maintained the peace and watched for signs of trouble. The Romans also built Roman towns, where they lived much as they lived in Rome.

Rome divided the lands into areas called provinces. Each province had a Roman governor.

The government sent its officials to distant cities and towns in the empire. They collected taxes, settled disputes, and made sure that Roman laws were obeyed.

Roman Roads

A stone called the Golden Milestone once lay in the center of the Roman Forum. It marked the spot where all the roads in the Roman Empire began. There is an old saying that all roads lead to Rome. In ancient Rome, this was true!

There were over 300 major roads throughout the empire . . . some 50,000

The Via Appia was a famous road begun in 312 BC.

One of the first roads was called the Via Salaria, or Salt Road, because traders used it to carry salt to Rome from the coast.

miles of them! Soldiers, traders, and travelers could move freely from Britain to Egypt.

For the most part, the roads were straight and well made. They could last 300 years without repairs!

Citizenship

Late in the empire, Rome gave citizenship to everyone except slaves and women. Many people could now say "*Civis Romanus sum*" ("I am a Roman citizen"). One Roman poet said the Romans had turned the entire world into Rome itself.

Latin

The Romans spoke a language called *Latin.* Latin spread throughout the empire and was the language used in law and in government. Latin gradually replaced many native languages and was the official language of the empire.

For hundreds of years after the empire fell, educated people read and wrote in Latin. Latin and Greek became the basis for words we still use in science and medicine.

Spanish, French, Italian, Portuguese, and Romanian all come from Latin. These are called the *Romance languages*. (Can you figure out why?) English is not a Romance language. But 25 percent of our words come from Latin roots or words.

Turn the page to learn how to speak Latin.

LATIN	MEANING	ENGLISH
Dent	Tooth	Dentist
Mar	Sea	Marine
Corp	Body	Corpse
Pater	Father	Paternal
Mater	Mother	Maternal
Totus	Whole	Total

Famous People

The ancient Roman world was full of rich and colorful characters. Some were renowned and helped unite the empire and accomplish great things. Some were tragic and failed to do great things. And others were . . . well . . . they were just plain awful!

Turn the page to meet some of the most memorable characters from ancient Rome.

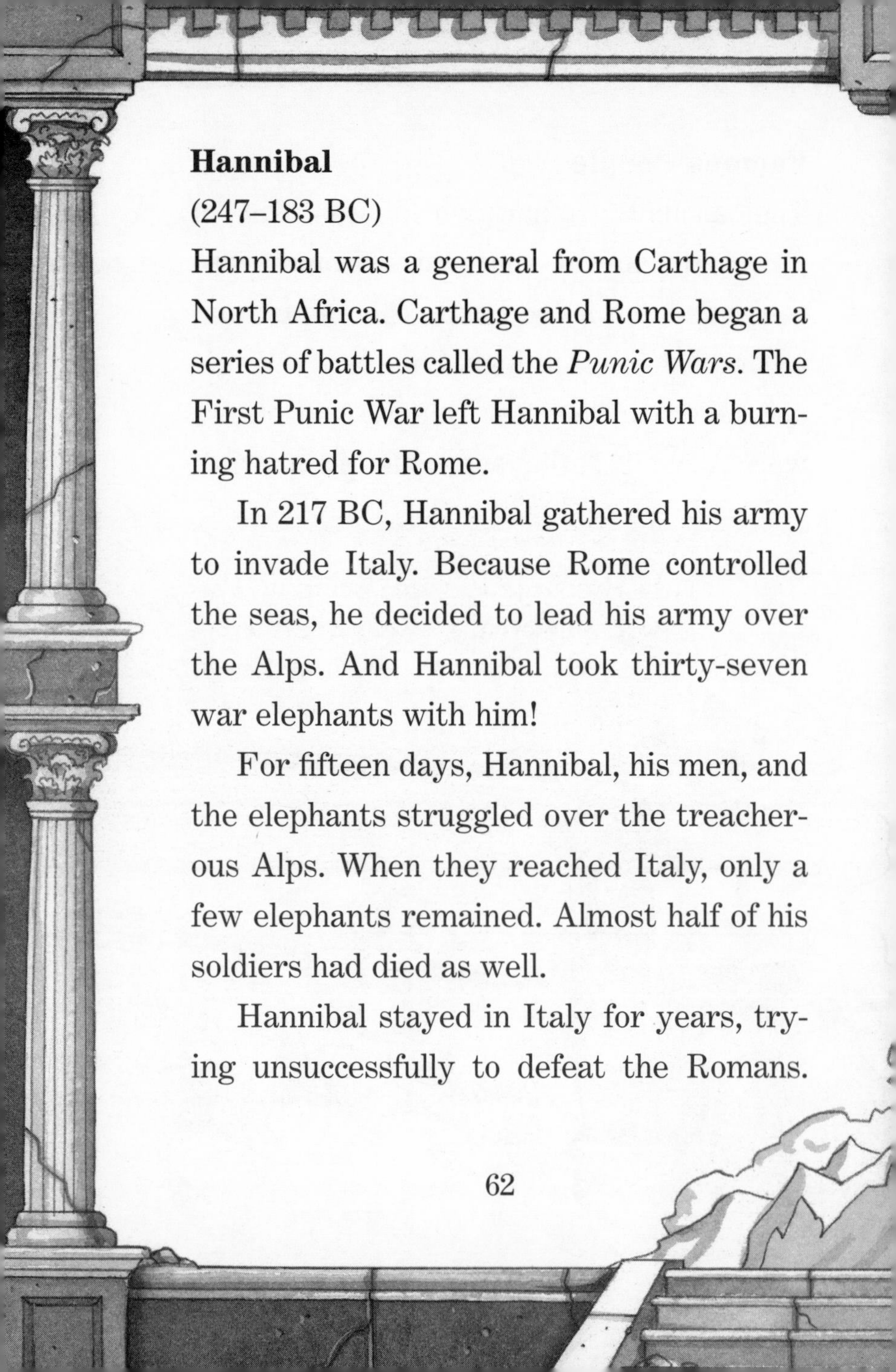

Hannibal

(247–183 BC)

Hannibal was a general from Carthage in North Africa. Carthage and Rome began a series of battles called the *Punic Wars*. The First Punic War left Hannibal with a burning hatred for Rome.

In 217 BC, Hannibal gathered his army to invade Italy. Because Rome controlled the seas, he decided to lead his army over the Alps. And Hannibal took thirty-seven war elephants with him!

For fifteen days, Hannibal, his men, and the elephants struggled over the treacherous Alps. When they reached Italy, only a few elephants remained. Almost half of his soldiers had died as well.

Hannibal stayed in Italy for years, trying unsuccessfully to defeat the Romans.

Eventually, years after Hannibal's death, the Romans attacked Carthage and burned it to the ground.

Julius Caesar
(100–44 BC)
Julius Caesar was a brilliant Roman general. After eight long years of fighting the Gauls, he returned in triumph to become ruler of Rome. Caesar ruled for five years. He was such a strong leader that many feared he wanted to be crowned king.

So on March 15, 44 BC, when Caesar went to give a speech in the Senate, danger was waiting. Several senators, including his close friends Brutus and Cassius, planned to kill him. They feared Caesar's power and did not want to be governed by a king.

As Caesar sat down, the men grabbed him around the neck and began stabbing him. They stabbed him twenty-three times. One writer said that Caesar looked at Brutus in disbelief and gasped, "You too, my child?" After Caesar's death, Rome was plunged into terrible civil war and chaos.

Octavian

(63 BC–AD 14)

Octavian became the first emperor of the Roman Empire. He was a great-nephew of Julius Caesar. In his will, Caesar made Octavian his adopted son.

After Caesar's murder, Octavian avenged his uncle by defeating Caesar's enemies. Then he seized control of the government. Octavian did not want to call himself an emperor, but he really was. In 27 BC, the Senate proclaimed Octavian *princeps,* or "first citizen." Octavian changed his name to *Augustus*, which means "respected one."

Augustus created order in the empire. He had beautiful buildings built all over Rome. Augustus said later that he had found a city of brick and changed it to a city of marble.

Cleopatra

(69–30 BC)

When she was eighteen, Cleopatra ruled Egypt with one of her brothers. But her brother forced her out of Egypt. Julius Caesar helped Cleopatra in her struggle, and she became queen of Egypt.

Caesar and Cleopatra fell in love. When Caesar returned to Rome, Cleopatra followed. After Caesar's murder, Cleopatra returned home.

But Cleopatra fell in love again . . . this time with Marc Antony, one of Caesar's strongest supporters. But Marc Antony and Octavian had become enemies. With Cleopatra's support, Antony went to war against Octavian. He was badly defeated in the Battle of Actium in 31 BC.

Antony committed suicide rather than

be put to death. Since Cleopatra had supported Antony, she knew she would be taken to Rome in chains and paraded through the streets. So she, too, took her own life. Some say she did so by the bite of a poisonous snake. Shortly afterward, Rome conquered Egypt.

Boudicca

(?–AD 60)

Boudicca (boo-DICK-uh) was the queen of the Iceni, a tribe in Britain. In AD 60, when the Romans taxed her land, Boudicca refused to pay any taxes at all.

As punishment, the Romans tied Boudicca and her daughters to posts and beat them. Boudicca was furious. She gathered an army and managed to capture three Roman towns. For three months, Boudicca and her army rampaged through the countryside. Thousands of people died.

The Roman governor sent for reinforcements. They badly defeated Boudicca's army. Boudicca realized she would pay with her life. She drank poison rather than allow herself to be captured by her enemies.

Caligula

(AD 12–41)

Caligula (kuh-LIG-yoo-luh) was born into a royal Roman family. The name Caligula actually means "tiny boot." Soldiers gave him this nickname as a child. (Caligula's real name was Gaius Julius Caesar Germanicus.)

Caligula behaved very badly when he was emperor. He killed anyone he wanted to. He rolled about on heaps of gold and drank pearls dissolved in vinegar. Once his army fought near the seashore. After the battle, Caligula ordered his soldiers to collect seashells. He told them this was their only reward for fighting.

Caligula wanted to make his horse, Incitatus, a consul. He even built a marble stall and draped Incitatus in purple blankets. (Purple was a royal color; the dye came from a rare snail.) Then Caligula demanded that everyone bow down to his horse.

Finally, Caligula built a temple to himself. He thought he was the god Jupiter. Fearful about the future of Rome, his own guards murdered him in AD 41. He was only twenty-nine.

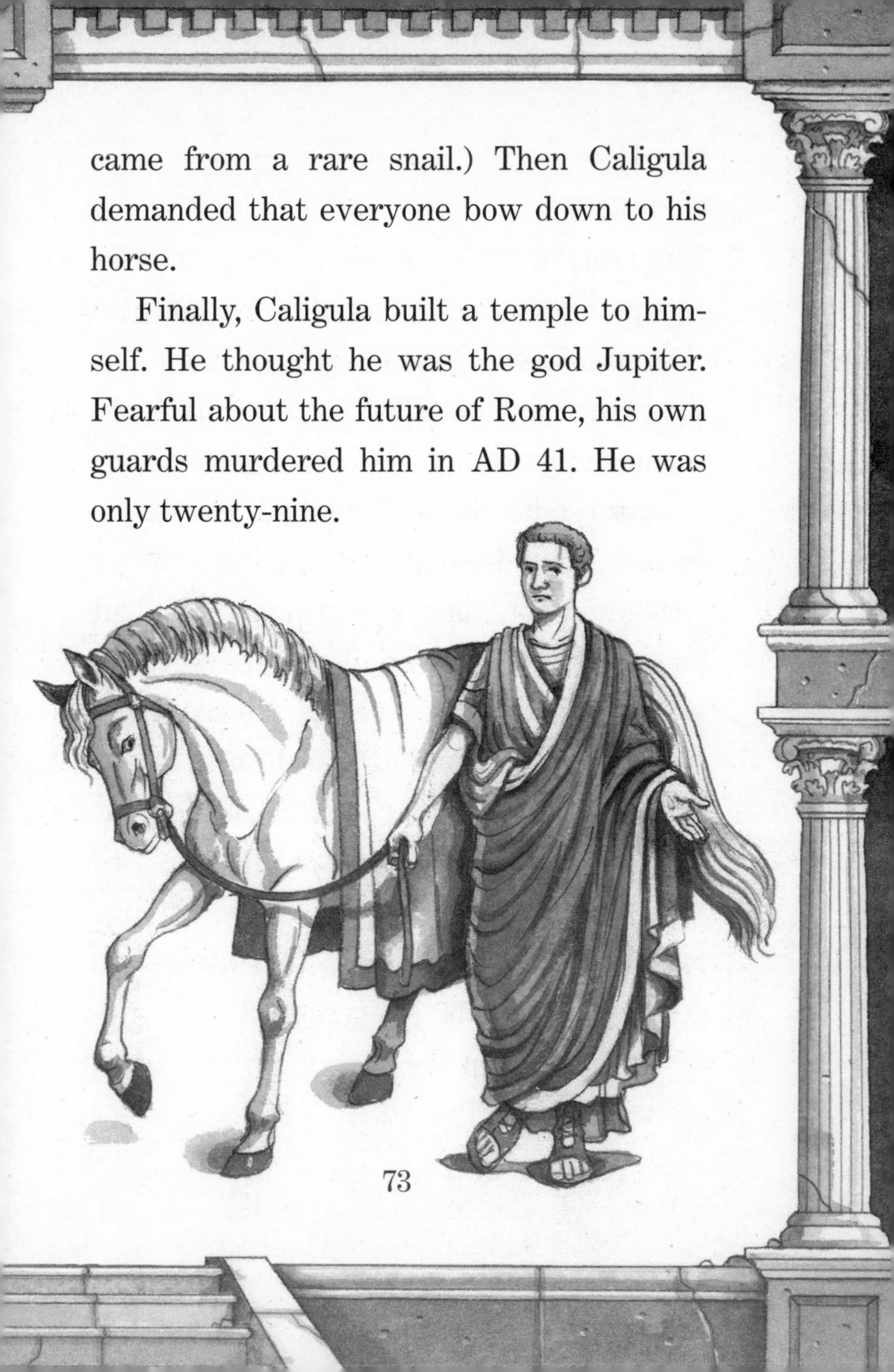

Nero

(AD 37–68)

Emperor Nero's mother was named Agrippina (a-gruh-PEE-nuh). She was also Caligula's sister. Some say Agrippina poisoned her husband, Claudius, so Nero could become emperor.

Nero felt his mother had too much power, so he decided to poison her. Nero's poison did not work on Agrippina. She had taken a bit every day and was immune.

Nero would not give up. He fixed the ceiling over his mother's bed so it would collapse. But it never did. So Nero sent Agrippina on a ride in a boat designed to sink. But Agrippina swam ashore. Finally, Nero ordered his soldiers to stab her to death. This time Nero succeeded!

Nero thought he was a great singer,

even though he actually wasn't. He forced people to attend his concerts.

The Romans grew to hate Nero. Knowing that he would lose his throne, Nero committed suicide. It is reported that his last words were "Oh, what an artist the world is losing."

5

Death in Pompeii

August 24, 79, promised to be a beautiful day in Pompeii. Pompeii was a pleasant Roman town on the slopes of Mt. Vesuvius overlooking the Bay of Naples. The daily life of Pompeii was like daily life in Roman towns everywhere.

As the sun rose, people began to stir. Bakers opened their bakeries to prepare bread for the day. They hitched up the small donkeys that turned the millstone. Slowly

the donkeys began walking around in circles, turning the wheel. After the grain was ground, the smell of baking bread filled the air.

At the forum, sleepy shopkeepers unbolted the shutters and doors to their shops. Women carrying offerings walked quietly to the nearby Temple of Jupiter. Businessmen and officials greeted each other on their way to work.

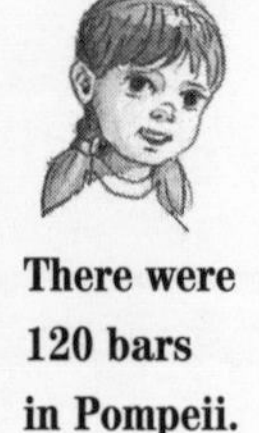

There were 120 bars in Pompeii.

Shoppers began to fill the streets carrying baskets of food and other goods. As in Rome, bars opened for the first customers of the day. Children played in the streets with tops and marbles.

At the public baths, men chatted as they washed themselves. Some exercised while others soaked lazily in the warm water. Slaves stood by with towels and fragrant oils.

Maybe some people talked about the small *tremors* in the earth that they'd felt for a few days. No one seemed concerned.

A tremor is a shaking.

Little tremors happened frequently. No one knew that by nightfall, Pompeii would be in terrible danger. Mt. Vesuvius was actually a dormant volcano, and it was waking up.

Dormant means "asleep."

A Cloud Like a Pine Tree

The story of what happened next came from an actual eyewitness. He was called Pliny (PLIN-ee) the Younger. Pliny was across the bay from Pompeii. He wrote down all he saw and heard.

Pliny watched in horror as the top of Mt. Vesuvius blew off. He wrote that an enormous cloud shaped like an Italian umbrella pine tree rose in the sky.

Italian umbrella pine trees grow all over Italy today.

The cloud loomed over Pompeii. Parts of it were white; other parts were dark with dirt and ash.

Volcanic rock called *pumice* (PUH-mis) rained down hard and fast. People tried to cover their heads with pillows or anything that was handy.

Suddenly the cloud blocked the sun. It grew as dark as night. Thick ash clogged everyone's nose and eyes. By now sixteen inches of pumice had fallen to the ground. Roofs began to collapse. A rotten-egg smell from sulfurous gas filled the air.

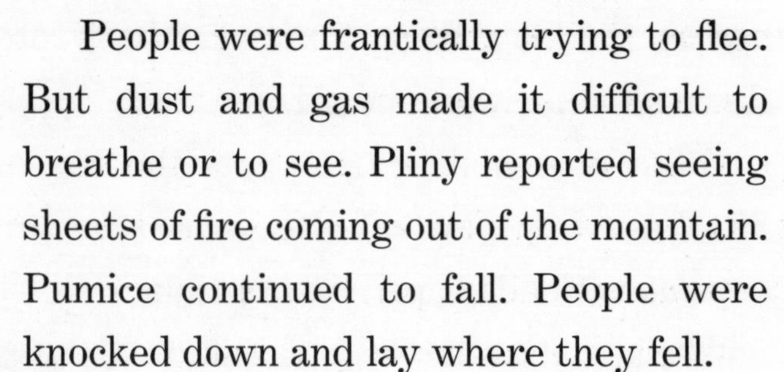

People were frantically trying to flee. But dust and gas made it difficult to breathe or to see. Pliny reported seeing sheets of fire coming out of the mountain. Pumice continued to fall. People were knocked down and lay where they fell.

Experts estimate over 2,000 people died.

Pliny reported that four days later, there were frequent earthquakes and lightning. As the hours passed, pumice piled up eight feet deep. The waters below the town boiled from the hot melted rock.

Pliny the Elder, Pliny the Younger's uncle, was a scientist who died because he refused to flee.

Amazingly, a few survivors staggered around the rubble searching for loved ones.

But Mt. Vesuvius had one last trick. Suddenly a huge surge of poisoned gas, ash, and rock raced down the mountain, destroying everything in its path. For two days afterward, ash continued to fall. Finally, the cloud disappeared. The volcano was settling down for another long sleep. Pompeii had ceased to exist.

6

Daily Life in a Roman Town

In 1710, a farmer was digging a well on the slopes of Mt. Vesuvius. His shovel struck large slabs of marble buried in the dirt.

Other people found out about the man's discovery. They remembered that the Roman cities of Herculaneum and Pompeii had been destroyed more than 1,600 years before. They concluded that the marble came from the ruins of the towns.

Over the years, people explored the area where the towns had been. Sometimes their digging damaged the sites. And if they found something valuable, they usually sold it.

Excavation means to uncover something by digging it up.

In 1860, an archaeologist named Giuseppe Fiorelli began the first proper *excavation* (eks-kuh-VAY-shun) of Pompeii.

Fiorelli removed tons of dirt that covered the city. He found remains of streets and buildings. Since then, teams of archaeologists have excavated and restored many streets and houses in Pompeii. This excavation gives us a great idea of what life was like in a typical Roman town thousands of years ago.

But Fiorelli also uncovered something else that was fascinating. During the eruption, people and animals were buried in ash. Rains compressed the ash around their bodies. Although the bodies decayed, the ash hardened to form a mold around the person or animal that died.

Fiorelli pumped plaster into the empty spaces inside the molds where the bodies had been. This turned them into plaster statues. Thanks to Fiorelli, we can see how and where many people actually died. Among the bodies was a beggar carrying his money box, a dog tangled in its rope,

Even their sandals were clearly defined.

In the Garden of the Fugitives, the remains of thirteen men, women, and children were found huddled together.

and a man who covered himself and his little girl with cushions. They are sad reminders of the victims of Mt. Vesuvius.

Pompeii

About 40 percent of the people in Pompeii were slaves.

When Mt. Vesuvius erupted in AD 79, 20,000 people lived in Pompeii. Shopkeepers, businessmen, and craftsmen lived next to rich Romans, who came to escape the noise and dirt of Rome.

Streets in Pompeii were lined with huge paving stones. Crossing them could

You can still see ruts cut by the carts into the paving stones.

be difficult. Shoppers crowded the narrow, dirty streets. Shopkeepers threw garbage onto the pavement. Gutters full of water ran on both sides of the roads. To cross from one side to the other, people had to walk carefully over raised stepping stones. And while they were crossing, they had to dodge carts and chariots.

As in all Roman cities, streets were divided into blocks called *insulae* (IN-sul-lay). Houses, shops, and bars filled almost every block. And every street had shrines for the gods. One insula that has been excavated has five houses with gardens, a bar, and four shops.

Insulae means "islands" in Latin.

Houses

Houses in Pompeii had white plastered fronts with bold red stripes running

There were no police in Pompeii. People often owned guard dogs.

along the bottom. Windows were often high, narrow slits to keep out burglars. Poor families usually crowded into one or two rooms on the street level.

A large fancy house was called a villa.

But many families lived in larger houses. In the middle of the house stood a central courtyard called an *atrium* (AY-tree-um). This is where the family greeted friends and set up family altars. Bedrooms or other rooms opened onto the atrium. Homes in Pompeii often had gardens behind the atrium. Families could sit and eat in the shade during hot weather.

At the House of Vettii, archaeologists have restored a beautiful small garden. It is carefully laid out with statues and fountains. In fact, every house in Pompeii seems to have had a garden of some sort. There were both flower and vegetable gardens. Archaeologists think this was common in Roman towns throughout the empire.

Roses and other beautiful flowers grew in the House of Vettii garden.

Furniture and Decoration

Houses in ancient Rome would look bare to us today. This was also true in Pompeii. Families did not own much furniture.

Rich families had woolen mattresses and beautiful bed covers.

Almost every house in Pompeii did have beds and couches where people sat, ate, and rested.

In addition, archaeologists have found tables, stools, and benches. These were usually made of bronze. Small bronze heaters called braziers (BRAY-zhurz) found in many rooms would burn charcoal for warmth in cold weather.

Light came from candles or oil lamps, like this one with a handle shaped like a horse's head.

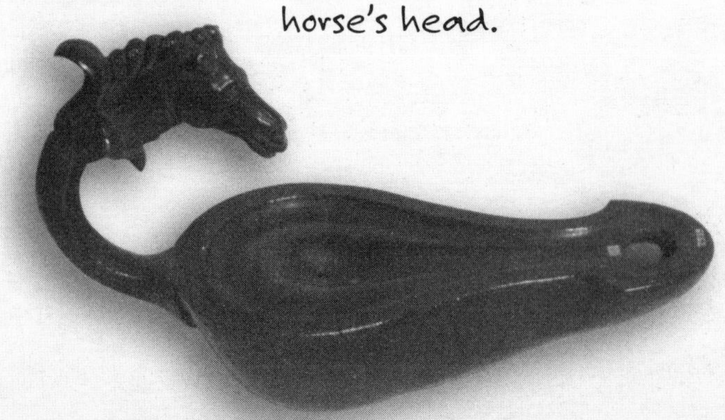

Many houses in Pompeii had beautiful murals painted on the walls. For example, in the House of Vetti, archaeologists uncovered murals in the atrium that depicted mythological scenes. People even had pictures of family members painted on their walls.

Family Meals

Romans enjoyed their food. Wealthy Romans wrote about it and talked about it. They even bragged about their cooks in letters to each other.

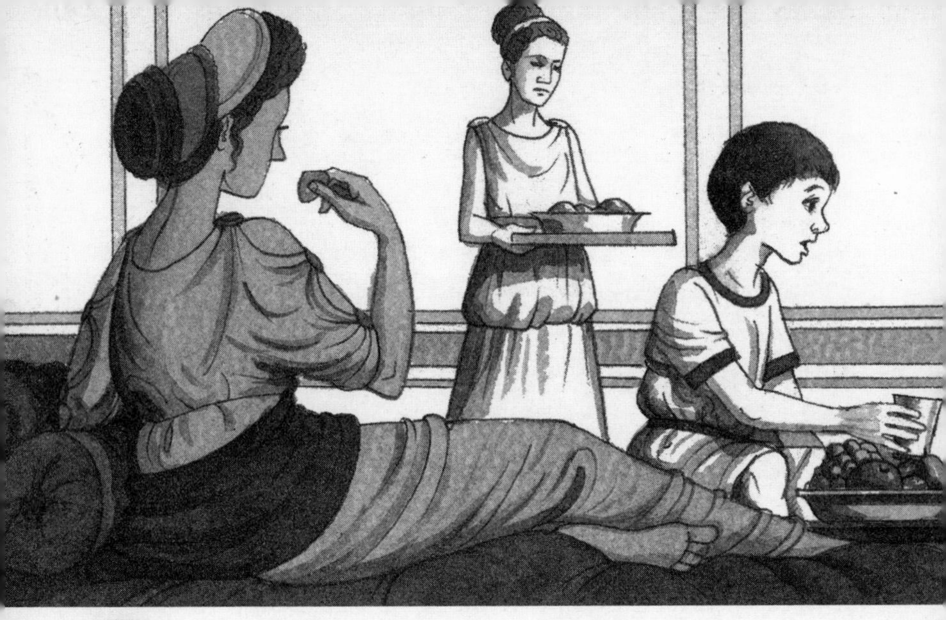

Since there was no chimney, smoke drifted out the window.

Except in poor families, slaves did all the cooking. They baked in brick ovens and hung their pots over a wood fire. In one kitchen in Pompeii, pots were found still hanging on the walls.

Families in Pompeii, like most Roman families, lay on couches when they ate. Each couch held three people. When people ate, they leaned on their left elbows and ate with their right hands.

Wall paintings in Pompeii show baskets of fruit, fish, rabbits, and vegetables. In a house in Herculaneum, the family was having lunch. When the volcano erupted, they left bread, eggs, cake, and fruit behind on the table.

This 2,000-year-old loaf of bread was discovered in a bakery oven!

Family Life

In the group of bodies found in the Garden of the Fugitives, one man is on his elbow. He seems to be gazing at the bodies of a woman and child nearby. Perhaps this was a father looking for the last time at his loved ones.

In Pompeii, as in the rest of the empire, family life was important. Families often lived together—grandparents, mothers, fathers, and children.

In early Rome, a father could legally kill his children if they seriously disobeyed him!

Fathers were the heads of their families. They arranged their daughters' marriages, educated their sons, served in the government, and attended to business.

When a child was born, a nurse placed the baby at its father's feet. Then the father picked the child up and held it in his arms. This showed that he accepted responsibility for the child.

When boys were sixteen, they got their first shave and a haircut. Then they exchanged their childhood togas for the plain togas worn by men. Girls married in their teens, usually to men who were much older.

Later in the empire, women could own land and run businesses.

Boys went to school, but girls were taught at home.

Entertainment

The Festival of Saturn lasted seven days.

Roman families enjoyed celebrating birthdays, weddings, and festivals. There were two theaters in Pompeii where audiences watched actors perform tragedies and comedies.

All the actors were men and wore masks.

As in Rome, the favorite entertainment in Pompeii took place in the amphitheater. Up to 20,000 people gathered there to watch gladiators fight to the death. The crowds grew so excited, riots and fights sometimes broke out.

Bodies of gladiators and a lady with fine jewelry lay near the amphitheater.

For fun, children and adults played games like knucklebones. They threw bones in the air and tried to catch as many as possible. Children played with balls, dolls, and marbles. They played board games as well.

This mural of knucklebones players was found in Herculaneum.

Dress

Men and boys also wore longer, draped robes called togas for more formal dress.

Roman men and boys wore short, belted tunics. Powerful Roman men wore tunics with purple stripes to show their importance. Tunics were made from linen in the summer and wool in the winter.

Girls wore short tunics as well. When they grew up, they wore a long tunic called a *stola*.

Rich women adorned themselves with beautiful jewelry. One armband found in Pompeii was in the form of a coiled snake. Women also used cosmetics and perfume. Archaeologists have discovered perfume bottles, combs, silver mirrors, and cosmetic jars.

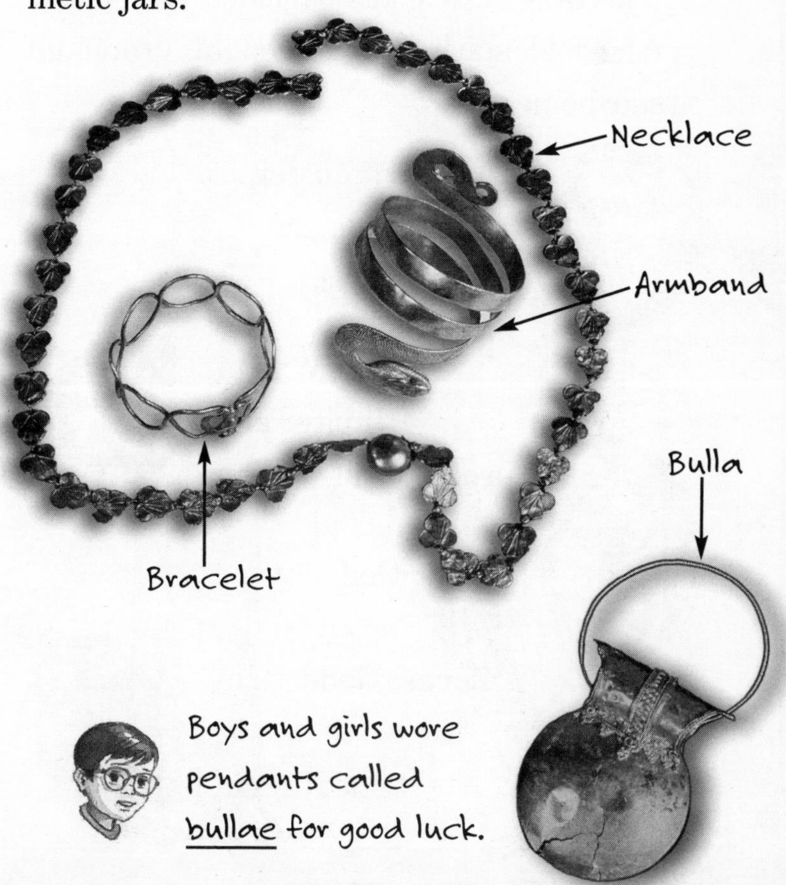

The Romans worshiped many gods and goddesses. Each family honored special household spirits they thought protected their homes.

Jupiter: Master of all the gods and god of the sky

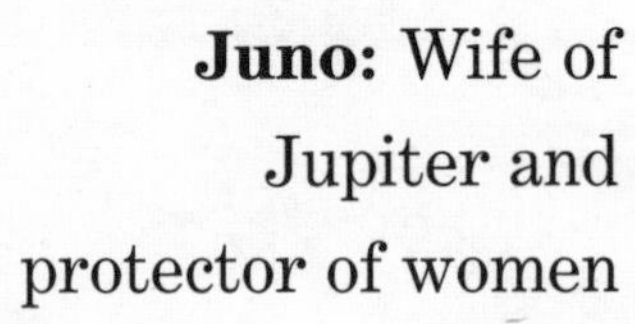

Juno: Wife of Jupiter and protector of women

Mars: God of war

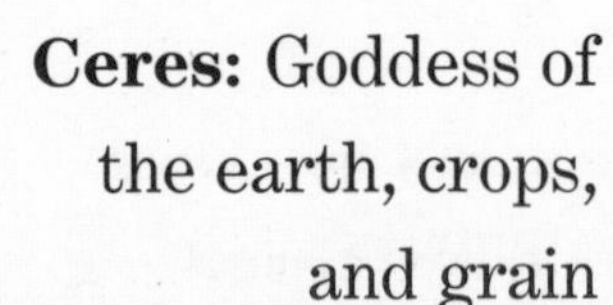

Ceres: Goddess of the earth, crops, and grain

Neptune: God of the sea

Venus: Goddess of love

Diana: Goddess of the moon and of hunting

Vesta: Goddess of the hearth and home

Mercury: Messenger of the gods

Vulcan: God of the underworld, fire, volcanoes, and metalworking

7

End of the Empire

Eventually, the Roman Empire began to weaken. The Romans fought among themselves for control of the government. Constant wars exhausted the army.

The empire became so weak, German tribes swept down and attacked the city of Rome itself. Most experts agree the Roman Empire ended in AD 476.

But the Romans left behind many gifts.

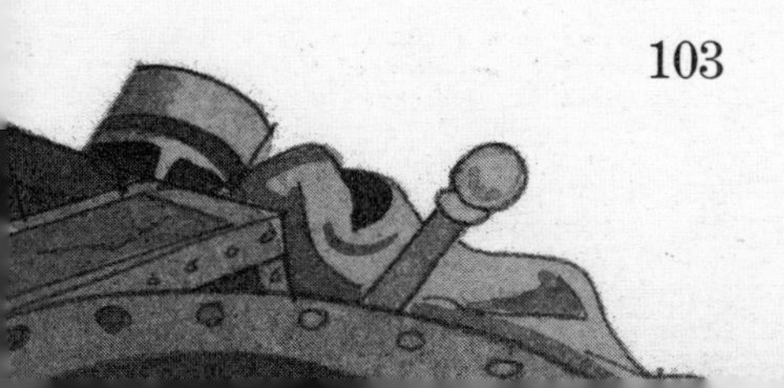

They taught us how to build roads, buildings, bridges, and cities. They created great works of art. They gave us ideas about how to govern and how to maintain order with a strong legal system. Our military leaders still study Julius Caesar's army and Roman military organization.

The Romans also left their language to the world. Latin has made the English language richer. Today we still read the works of great Roman writers and thinkers. And today we still marvel at their wisdom.

When we see statues of famous Roman leaders, we are often struck by their strong, serious faces. They look like powerful people. They look like men who could rule an empire.

Doing More Research

There's a lot more you can learn about ancient Rome and Pompeii. The fun of research is seeing how many different sources you can explore.

Books

Most libraries and bookstores have lots of books about ancient Rome and Pompeii.

Here are some things to remember when you're using books for research:

1. You don't have to read the whole book.
Check the table of contents and the index to find the topics you're interested in.

2. Write down the name of the book.

When you take notes, make sure you write down the name of the book in your notebook so you can find it again.

3. Never copy exactly from a book.

When you learn something new from a book, put it in your own words.

4. Make sure the book is nonfiction.

Some books tell make-believe stories about ancient Rome. Make-believe stories are called *fiction.* They're fun to read, but not good for research.

Research books have facts and tell true stories. They are called *nonfiction.* A librarian or teacher can help you make sure the books you use for research are nonfiction.

Here are some good nonfiction books about ancient Rome and Pompeii:

- *Ancient Rome* by Peter Connolly
- *Ancient Rome*, History in Stone series, by Sarah Eason
- *Famous Men of Ancient Rome: Lives of Julius Caesar, Nero, Marcus Aurelius and Others* by John H. Haaren and A. B. Poland
- *Life in Ancient Rome*, Kingfisher Knowledge series, by Simon Adams
- *Pompeii . . . Buried Alive!*, Step into Reading series, by Edith Kunhardt
- *Pompeii: Lost and Found* by Mary Pope Osborne
- *Rome Antics* by David Macaulay

Museums

Many museums have exhibits on ancient Rome. These places can help you learn more about life in ancient Rome.

When you go to a museum:

1. Be sure to take your notebook!

Write down anything that catches your interest. Draw pictures, too!

2. Ask questions.

There are almost always people at a museum who can help you find what you're looking for.

3. Check the museum calendar.

Many museums have special events and activities just for kids!

Here are some museums with exhibits about ancient Rome and Pompeii:

- Getty Museum, Los Angeles, California
- The Metropolitan Museum of Art, New York City, New York
- Michael C. Carlos Museum, Emory University, Atlanta, Georgia
- University of Pennsylvania Museum of Archaeology and Anthropology, Philadelphia, Pennsylvania

Videos and DVDs

There are some great nonfiction videos and DVDs about ancient Rome and Pompeii. As with books, make sure the videos and DVDs you watch for research are nonfiction!

Check your library or video store for these and other nonfiction videos and DVDs about ancient Rome and Pompeii:

- *Ancient Rome* from Schlessinger Media
- *Colosseum: A Gladiator's Story* from Discovery Channel
- *Pompeii: The Last Day* from Discovery Channel
- *The Roman Empire in the First Century* from PBS
- *Seven Wonders of Ancient Rome* from Discovery Channel

The Internet

Many Web sites have lots of facts about the Romans. Some also have games and activities that can help make learning about ancient Rome and Pompeii even more fun.

Ask your teacher or your parents to help you find more Web sites like these:

- www.historyforkids.org/learn/romans/history/earlyrepublic.htm
- www.historylearningsite.co.uk/roman_army_and_warfare.htm
- www.historyonthenet.com/Romans/society.htm
- www.members.aol.com/Donnclass/Romelife.html
- www.roman-empire.net/children

Software and CD-ROMs

Software and CD-ROMs often mix facts with fun activities.

Here are some software programs and CD-ROMs that will help you learn more about ancient Rome:

- *Ancient Lands*
  from Microsoft
- *Life in Ancient Rome*
  from Discovery School

Good luck!

Index

Photos courtesy of:

© **Alinari Archives/CORBIS** (p. 19). © **Archivo Iconografico, S.A./CORBIS** (cover, p. 29). **Art Resource, NY** (p. 99 top). © **Bettmann/CORBIS** (p. 32). **Statue of Cicero (106–43 BC), Roman, 1st century BC (marble)/ © Ashmolean Museum, University of Oxford, UK/ Bridgeman Art Library** (p. 17). © **Seamus Culligan/ ZUMA/CORBIS** (p. 28). **Mark Douet/Taxi/Getty Images** (p. 105). **Werner Forman/Art Resource, NY** (p. 57). © **Free Agents Limited/CORBIS** (p. 30). **The Granger Collection, New York** (p. 21). **Erich Lessing/Art Resource, NY** (pp. 86, 89, 93, 95, 97). **Bruno Morandi/ Robert Harding World Imagery/Getty Images** (pp. 79, 85). **Gold bulla from the House of Menander, Pompeii, 79 AD/Museo e Gallerie Nazionali di Capodimonte, Naples, Italy/Bridgeman Art Library** (p. 99 bottom). **North Wind Picture Archives** (p. 15). **Scala/Art Resource, NY** (pp. 37, 91). **R. Sheridan/ANCIENT ART & ARCHITECTURE COLLECTION, LTD.** (pp. 88, 90). **Vanni/Art Resource, NY** (p. 27). © **Ruggero Vanni/ CORBIS** (p. 34). © **K. M. Westermann/CORBIS** (p. 96). © **Roger Wood/CORBIS** (p. 35).

PAUL COUGHLIN